MW00364354

Gravesend

*The publisher gratefully acknowledges the support of the Leslie Scalapino Memorial Fund for Poetry, which was established by generous contributions to the University of California Press Foundation by Thomas J. White and the Leslie Scalapino– O Books Fund.*

COLE SWENSEN

# Gravesend

 University of California Press    Berkeley  Los Angeles  London

University of California Press, one of the most distinguished university presses in the United States, enriches lives around the world by advancing scholarship in the humanities, social sciences, and natural sciences. Its activities are supported by the UC Press Foundation and by philanthropic contributions from individuals and institutions. For more information, visit www.ucpress.edu.

University of California Press
Berkeley and Los Angeles, California

University of California Press, Ltd.
London, England

© 2012 by The Regents of the University of California

Library of Congress Cataloging-in-Publication Data

Swensen, Cole.
    Gravesend / Cole Swensen.
    p. cm. — (New California poetry ; 36)
    ISBN 978-0-520-27317-7 (pbk. : acid-free paper)
    I. Title.
    PS3569.W384G73    2012
    811'.54—dc23                                      2011041841

Manufactured in the United States of America

21   20   19   18   17   16   15   14   13   12
10   9   8   7   6   5   4   3   2   1

The paper used in this publication meets the minimum requirements of ANSI/NISO Z39.48-1992 (R 2002) (*Permanence of Paper*).

To
Hilton Juul Swensen, 1899–2001,
Scharlotte Swensen, 1905–1999,
and
Charles Clemens Swensen, 1928–2010

# Contents

Gravesend

ONE

# HAVE YOU EVER SEEN A GHOST?

# Echo Body

I sat on an edge       and a gate clicked shut       and the world thus recalled

a man who walked      into a churchyard, if a man      closed his hand, you'd
call it a fist, but that was not      the fence      immense, the single note

upon note      that breaks in the sun      because what walked on
walked so lightly across the burning stones      that we gave in

# If

the horse was white     and the green hill opened out          an animal          the lamp
of any landscape   where the angle of incident light is an index     and on the grey ridge

on the other side       any animal so largely domestic     a large white dog, for instance
coming out of the sea alone    would be alarming   with its head in your lap like a window

# Sometimes the Ghost

Sometimes the ghost arrives before the body is gone and the breath which will one day white, there will be walls, or illness may be the cause and cause the ghost to crawl up inside, a bright

illness, when the eyes go, and the ghost walks around looking like you, and we talk quietly, and she says things I remember your saying, but at the time they were out of context and made no sense, and now I look around the room that fits. And I walk across the room with my eyes closed

# Etymology

Ghost: *gast,* as in soul-sprite, breath-life, sliced    wreath    of a waning break    it rears
from all over        has been called the back-comer    the night-child        the guest

of lack-print and glass-phoid        of shatter-this all the way back            unto 1385
when the word was first connected to what wanders off from the body    an aerial scarring

on the surface        most words for ghost are pieces    of mica that carefully layered
will make a window        out of fire. It's cold        and the faces at the window

do what faces usually do            they open onto                a genetic history
that looks up suddenly and     it's the eyes everyone says    you can't say that's not alive

# A Ghost

erodes the line between being and place     becomes the place of being time     and so
the house turns in the snow     is why a ghost always has the architecture of a storm

The architect tore down room after room     until the sound stopped.    A ghost is one
among the ages at the edge of a cliff     empty sails on the bay     even when a ship

or the house moves off in fog     asks you out loud     to let the stranger in

# He Who Was

was an ordinary man    who turned to light a stove    who shadow-flew-on-wall

will nothing there awake    like anybody else    who, picking up the mail

and so the shattered half—    I watched a man    walking down a hill

or in the garden of the dark    watched I his veil    and saw within

who now straightened up    with the shears    in one hand and the zinnias

in the other    the corner of the eye    is an enormous room

# Varieties of Ghost

Phantom     shade     specter     wraith     haint     and then the *revenant*     that
who has come back     who is precisely what     fond emptiness     that the errant is

the error that faces you     and is not so empty, now it turns     back and faces you
that remembered you     that forgot to say     something     was forgotten because the day

arrayed itself     in overlapping screens     a superimposition of scenes in which
someone a century later crossing a street     turns around too quickly     and there you are

a rip in the air     through which the endless endlessness     that replaces us     calmly stares

# Ajar

He emerged from a doorway, she came out of the mirror, he simply appeared,
I turned around and there she was on the hearth, the carpet, the stairs. Ghosts
always look like they're alone which is to say, are seen one by one, and so the
field extends right there in the room or a vast plateau among wind, holding
out her hand, she came in from the garden and held out her hand as if to say
take it, pointing to the small object therein, which turned out to be a tooth

# The Ghost Is in Itself

a boundary, is that which distinguishes    the past from the after    which is simply
the fact that    a ghost itself can never be older    than the fact that a dead

child is instantly    older than any of us will ever be    more widely a tendency
to recur, which is a kind of clock    that stopped    the endless circling

that traces a circle    there in the dust on the floor    where sunlight sketches
an hourglass    was on again, the *revenant,* but no    time only seems circular to those

indentured to the sun    something about gravity that    while a long line stretches out
the errant of the heart  you know they cannot swerve  or perhaps the notion of cyclical time

is based on the spherical earth    if you lived anywhere else    you'd never see them again

# The End of Antiquity

There was a certain point at which    the story changed       from that of the living who
traveled to the underworld and back          and became instead      one of the dead

who came from the land of the dead        and could not return      is a grieving. Why
are we frightened      by doorways; why is there a fear      especially made for the sound

of a door   or a year   or a stare    Fear is an aperture      but also a ligature. Something
deep inside the house      swings shut       and they start to describe it as something else

# According to Scripture

Or at times against its will, the ghost is called back, even wrenched, from its treading-space
by a voice, don't        even think of it, maybe hurtled        toward a light inside of which

a certain play of grief and sand        had been trying to forget        as had the ghost
in 1 Samuel 28:13 who said "I have been torn    from the touch      I am blind, and I flinch

and had forgotten how the world in which you live is so limited in its range of visible light"

# More Miracula

They say upon the death          a brighter than the sun          and closed it like a mind
but a sky fell down in gold          made the sky of rope          and she climbed slowly up

to everything in sight   this is the story of a saint   is broken   raking   is raked up and torn

The storm was my fault

and put the lantern down.

Sister Tortgith claimed she saw a woman she couldn't name rising into the sky one morning, and three days later the Mother Superior died; it was that simple, and as she herself lay dying three years later, the same woman appeared before her and, standing at the open window, negotiated with her for her "date of release." There was a bit of an argument, at least it sounded like that to the chronicler, who, granted, heard only one side, but it was just a short time later that Tortgith was "delivered from the bonds and infirmity of the flesh."

# Going Home

there came unto him   who said that his horse  was one among the left
was walking down       in a shroud of bees       would make a man

crawl home and hide inside his eyes            one William of Glos
the horse still alight        said, and you without heir       said, you

who harbor here          this story          is told in many versions
and though the place remains the same, the century shifts    as if a man

slipped     on his own name       and became   a repetition in tongues

# The Hellequin's Hunt

Mist lay in the valley as we set out       shroud around          and all along the river
started taking shape  a phalanx of approach   suddenly agape while wholly in our sight

we saw      And here the chronicler      visibly shaking        though questioned for days
could not stop crying, claiming   they passed us in the forest  a contingency of corpses

hundreds and hundreds strong   and the din of their wailing    the cacophony of armor
and others in chains        as they might have been in ages       an army of entirety

winding endlessly through the woods        with no enemy but eternity         throughout
the Middle Ages                 armies of ghosts were heard on stormy nights pounding

their spectral steeds through a wind of howling dogs      led by the deadest of them all
and followed by the thousands        it was a time in which        a ghost could be

indeterminate in number      and in crowds      swept across        whole counties awash
that look           from a distance like fog                though some say no

God said a lightning strike
                    counts every thing alive
                              and arrives
                                        in a long winding shroud
of rhythmic footsteps wrapped and wrapping      all in a white instant of insistent lime

## The Gesta

But when they saw the wound     but when was full of hounds    a pack, grounded
can trace a grain of salt    back to its star     that could not be staunched

was an arrow thrown by hand     and though they'd never seen him before
they knew his name   and so the town was saved. Before the modern age, the ghost story

was not a genre as such    but was something that accrued     not without alarm
yet with a kind of trust    she took the wound without the arm and wore it as a past

# Who Only Living

lived alone        an image held, owned,        and so *on we thought*

of the image as it solely   presented the soul in perpetuity   fifteenth century
and because he was invisible, a tracery        and they in the circle felt

on the backs of their necks   and the signs made of hands   copied the circle
which prevented the fire from reaching the mind    the all-of-a-flying, there

in the image of a man alive    who nonetheless died    all over our hands

is more often the shape of something material        a dog, a bird, a friend
which is to say  to say 'invisible' means not to recognize  for sight is always second

to a subtler precedent        and were he to look different now, intermittently, to

say you would have known him        is always ambiguous        a grey scale
that one might thwart across a hearth   yet to undertake    is to raise the body up

a friend, a bird, at first        someone else        called out        and gestured if

like rain on a lake, like wind        can never be painted        is constrained
to its effects        on leaves        on trees        on things        in the world

# The Ghost Story

began as a collision     between what the Church said     and what everybody saw
in the sky between     the trees if a cloud     could have taken on

legible form     you could have lost your way     it could have followed you home

And so the concept of a ghost was itself    something that returned    that drifted back
from an earlier system of belief    for had it been known that the dead are not at peace

what would Christ have said    had held    his children in a silver fever for the voyage
to death was a bridge and not a river   with a gate that swings   one way in patient only

one lonely moment in which    if the moment falters, alters    you almost sever
but the Church fathers could never     quite convince them of this

# History

In Augustine's time it was more likely the living      who reached out to touch

nothing, which broken-hearted      the dead were thought      to know everything
suspended in the middle          of the story          she would wake up stretching

her arms out so far they would hurt                  and still the dead remain
indeterminate and cold          and Augustine had to tell them                  no

and                  God is slow and                  the face you see at the window
is your own                  from a long way off          which is what it's like

to be dead. Augustine went    so far as to write an essay titled *How to Help the Dead*
which held    a candle in the burning hand      as the cradle      went up in snow

# What Ghosts

want has greatly changed across the ages.　　　　　They used to want forgiveness
or understanding　　　how the prayers worked down　　　into the interstices; they once

stood beside insomniacs　　　speaking softly almost chanting　　　　　bring me
who's demanding　　　another entry　　　but our own　　　ghosts, the recent ones

don't ask much　　　they just waver on the verges, a doorsill　　　can empty them
and the room beyond　　　they do not want　　　and this is the cause of great pain

# Interview Series 1

*Have you ever seen a ghost?*
*Were you frightened?*

Have you ever seen a ghost?
. . . It depends on what you mean
by seen
(pause)
there were a few times
or maybe somewhere in between
who passed through a doorway, always the same. My wife felt it too. No, it's not that I
*didn't* see him; what I'm calling into question here is the notion of seeing.

Were you frightened?
No, it was more alarming than threatening—the latter is sheerly physical; whereas, the
former also engages the intellect.

I'm going to ask as many people as possible in the coming week whether they've ever seen
a ghost, and if so, if it frightened them.

Have you ever seen a ghost?
Well, yes . . . just glimpses—something out of the corner of my eye, something crossing a
room; I didn't exactly see it, and it was oddly colorless.

Were you frightened?
No, not particularly.

Initially, I was thinking that 60 to 70% of the people I asked would say that they had
seen a ghost; so far, two people, two yeses, so my statistics are overflowing at 100%. And
yet, would you have thought it, just looking around the room? Would you have thought
that over 70% of these people who look so untroubled have ever seen anything that they
couldn't in any way explain? They don't look like it to me. And do they speak of it? And
will they if I ask them? And if they do speak of it, will they start to "look like it"?

Have you ever seen a ghost?

No. No . . . but . . . hmmm . . . *seen*—it's a complex word. What I mean is that I've perceived presences. Yes, people I've known, people I've loved very much; you can feel them there, still with you. You can talk to them. No, no, of course they never answer.

Do they frighten you?

No, of course not; I love them.

I asked these three people about their hesitancy around the words "see" and "seen," and one replied that it's a problem of language, which is to say, a ghost cannot be spoken. Perhaps we all see them; they're all around us, but can't be shared. They're a certain secret, like all the unsayable. Remains a private searcher in a corner. Like true love, which can never, though not through lack of effort, be stated. A secret,
a real one, is necessarily something
you tried so hard (and failed) (in every imaginable way) to say: I really don't think I believe in ghosts, but

once I was sleeping downstairs in a house, and in the bedroom above me, all night long, I heard the woman who lived there pacing back and forth, and I thought, oh what a shame, Nina must be worried; she's not sleeping, and in the morning, I mentioned it, saying that I hoped everything was all right, and she said, oh yes, I slept just fine—that was our ghost you heard.

"Our." It's a personal thing, an alliance, and precious, and private: a ghost is a form of privacy. And no, I wasn't frightened because by then it was over, and it didn't need believing.

Have you ever seen a ghost?

No, sorry (real apology in the tone). Once I thought I did, but it was the morning after a night of telling ghost stories, so, really . . . What did it look like? Oh, it was just the way the clothes had been thrown over an open closet door, and there was this strange face on top. The face? Well, yes, that was the part that didn't quite fit.

Did it frighten you?
Very much.

It's meaningless to ask if ghosts are real—they have an effect in the world. They work. Can you say that the fright was real and yet that what caused it was not?

Have you ever seen a ghost?
No.
Does that frighten you?

We tell ghost stories because we need to grieve in proper names, and we need to pass it on with the name released. So most are signed "Anonymous." And most of us never mention the ghosts we see.

Have you ever seen a ghost?
No, never. *Sigh.* Who knows? Sometimes I think they're all around us; I mean, so all around us they're simply the background. We don't see air either, or wind. We live in them.

Which makes of them houses, which is why, increasingly throughout the centuries, it's houses that are haunted, and all houses are haunted (we all dream of becoming something that someone else could inhabit), which gives us a place to live.

And yes, throughout all time.

Have you ever seen a ghost?
Yes, a few. They were all in houses.
Were you frightened?

| who came with them | who then within, could slip | as you watch out a window or in |
| crossing a street | it's particularly | in the proximity |
| of things passing | a man driving too fast | answered |

with a body like water, a light

grey said to have a center

Have I ever seen a ghost? Yes, just last week. It was in a mirror; he was climbing the stairs. Of course, I swung around, and of course, there was nothing there.

Mirrored share. In what falls, what calls and in what state does the stain of the reflected   you cheated   you stared   no, I   and was left there

Have you ever seen a ghost?
Yes, I see them all the time. They have nothing to do with death—they're often quite alive, often on a train, or even in the bus, someone I know perfectly well, someone I know is hundreds, or even thousands, of miles away, will get on the train and look right through me.

Have you ever seen a ghost?
No, no, no! (laughing, hands up in "stop" position, quite briefly, all lightly) No.
Though
I have sensed

that I was staying with a friend and the *Bible* disappeared
that the window turned black where touched by the hand
that I heard all night the bolt being drawn
that I sang
Have you ever seen a ghost?

I was once shown around a medieval church by a very kind, very elderly clergyman, and when I mentioned him to the woman in the church's gift shop, she said, "Oh him again! He's been dead for years; I do so wish he'd give up."

No, I've never seen one, but my husband has—a distraught woman in a bright red dress running along the balcony of an empty theater—she raced headlong into the night-watchman and passed right through him, who never even saw her.

No, I've never seen one, but I've heard one. He'd knock on the ceiling and rant in Latin. Was I frightened? No, but I got very tired of it.

In fact, ghosts are more often something heard, either as in "I've never seen one, but my brother has, and told me about it" or "It depends upon what you mean by 'seeing'—  for instance, I once walked into an empty house
and heard someone pacing all night long.   I once heard a house   and it sounded like someone else.

Have you ever seen a ghost?
Well, not *seen,* but once as a child I answered the phone
and my grandfather said hello and asked to speak to my mother. I went to get her but she refused to answer because he was dead.

# Walking Through

I was walking through my grandfather called it was a long way across he said
I ran like mad it was his I knew the house was alone I knew the face that held
had opened the door I had known I had wanted on hearing his own and ran
back up the hill as I slammed the door and then I slammed the door

A ghost is a hearing is a calling and every gesture that builds the pressure
that then through unknowing becomes in pieces the inner ether so larger
grows the mansion and larger grows the wind, undid, and the child who ran
up the hill is an older man telling a story that is simply a story he lived

# A Face

is always a ghost    it's what we lost    on a ship   or forest   or Everest   or once
every face    is the ghost of an instant.    Behind every face    other faces pass

like actors behind a screen    like time, they go from right to left    like time
they're heading west.   Will one along a crowded road    become or seem to be

all of them, and they unfold;    a face is lined    with and within its own
dawn now    and in particular, the eyes    far from being   windows on the soul

are handed down  and must be worn   exactly as received   and must be returned

# Toward the End

of the 17th century    the fine white hand      became a category of ghost all its own
floating, it formed              almost a cornerstone         keystone        deployed

and precisely hovering at the base of the throat       that vulnerable notch     etched
in air   is where it thrives, arriving  with all its vaults exposed   it was a woman's hand

greatly elongated    we never wanted, etc.     up to the elbow       and very rarely
the entire woman     followed, floating across the room     two-thirds of them known

to their percipients    holding   a glass  of water or mirror    or the hand died alone

# The Beginnings of the Modern Era

It wasn't until the ghost story became a genre        that ghosts became strangers

denied as they were    by a Romantic flagrance so      stylized it found itself poised
on the tip of a letter opener        and the man holding it       in his hand

silhouetted      from the back      on a promontory    over a crevasse, which makes
his sister die of music       or the ghost is reduced       to an overpowering smell

of the sea    and only she can hear it:    what we've inherited    fletcher of tongues
thin in the wind who blinded by now     a ghost in fingers   is touching them empty

of all its burning   And we claim we never knew them living   which gets lost in living
and thus the phaeton stopped to pick him up     and went on to plunge over the cliff

just as it had done in all its lost          every night for the past fifty years
the ghost ship         the phantom train         the cathedral fear

and how right we are    to claim it isn't ours      though it leaves them stranded
or we abandon     or we, a screw     in a door nailed shut.       It isn't our fault

# Fairy Tale

It is wrong said the ghost        to be astonished at anything      as everything
is identical        given the right angle                  and sometimes the ghost

steps out from behind a tree        and the wolves go away.    She sat at the edge
of the playground and finished the story:    "The bird flew up    into the rafters

and landed there        looking almost natural"            Sometimes a forest
replaces the house                  but it should not be confused with the children

and the ghost                should not be mistaken for snow              though
he will tell you        that is not what I meant                  to do to you

TWO

# HOW DID GRAVESEND GET ITS NAME?

# Ghost Stories

## Defoe's Story

It took place in London at the end of the 17th century—a man was spending the evening at home, thinking often of a friend of his, a woman who was very ill, worrying about her, hoping she would live, when there was a knock on the door, and she entered, looking fine, thriving in fact, and sat down in a normal way and began a normal conversation, though she seemed a little more serious than usual until he began to cry, at which she continued quietly, discussing things of the soul, aspects of time, and he began to sob, and she continued speaking quietly, as he sobbed and sobbed, and when he finally looked up she was gone.

This story is not unusual and belongs to a subgenre in which the dead person seems to drop in on a few old friends on the way out, giving no indication that he or she has died, but stays and speaks, saying the clear water at the bottom of my hand will make a turn and my hand will go bottomless like a mirror forgets my face at the slightest glance there was a man standing beside

the clear water    pooled in the rock beneath a tree. The bright leaves    tore up the light

you would have seen  that he was part of the light   and asked him to help me climb down

## Le Fanu's Story

Sheridan Le Fanu offers a variation on this story in which the whole family hears a carriage arrive late at night, just at the time that (they later learn) their older daughter has died miles away. Even the dogs start barking, and they all clearly hear the folding down of the carriage stairs, but when they open the door, the courtyard is empty, and the dogs recoil in fear. So that the sight

of anyone in an unexpected place   so that the voice    now traveling alone out on its own
on a quiet day     I saw a friend I knew to be in Japan     I once saw my sister on a train

Sometimes it's only a strong resemblance, and you wonder if the person in question hasn't
had a close call, crossing the street with an absent mind, or walked out of a building just
moments before it blew up. Caught a cab on the corner & never knew. It happens every
day. We are made

in a thin thread          or of the line incised       into the pane     which may be only
a photograph   she said, whenever I look at a photograph, I see     not the man who died
years ago   but the one who will     one day as he's simply    looking out the window


## James' Story

In Henry James' version, an unnamed narrator discovers she has two good friends who've
had the same experience—a woman whose father came to her in a gallery in Italy as he
was dying in New York, and a man whose mother showed up in his rooms in Cambridge
just after she'd died. Determined that her two similarly-gifted friends should meet, she
makes numerous plans, but oddly, something always comes up to thwart them. Finally,
after she has become engaged to the male friend, our narrator decides that she really must
arrange this meeting, so she fixes up something so simple that it cannot fail. However, at
the last minute, she finally gets it: these two are destined to fall in love—there's really no
other possibility—and so she herself, and through subterfuge, prevents this last attempt.
Last because, by sheer coincidence, her female friend dies that night. In the morning,
overcome with guilt and remorse, the woman tells her lover what she has done, but he
declares, "That's not possible! She came to my rooms just before midnight!" The woman
insists that it must have been her ghost, while the man insists that she was alive. They
finally agree to disagree and get on with their lives. Except that the woman notices a
change in him, and one week before their wedding, gently declares that she knows that he
has been keeping up a liaison with her dead friend ever since that fatal night, and though
he denies it, he doesn't do so very vigorously, and allows her to break off their engagement.

Needless to say, neither ever marries.

And as it so often is with James, we are never sure if the ghost occurred, or if the woman was not simply eaten up by a jealousy engendered by her guilt, or, much more likely, by a different jealousy, a jealousy for that other world, which her obsession with that detail of her friends' lives tells us she preferred to her friends all along.


James' version is unusual, too, in that it's the only ghost story I know in which a ghost is genetic, a kind of corner-of-the-eye that just can't stop in time    and heard the other arrive though way across town        or felt a line drawn taught        and could not respond

although a light comes on        all on its own        every day at just that time        time they say, is stone. I once had a heart      made of string        and hung myself, my love

# A Good Friend

Edith Wharton, a good friend of James   said a woman is a mansion   and half the rooms
unentered   and lost   in the rooms   it's the soul that splits   into times

you don't recognize   that the soul squanders   or is squandered   by curtains
she couldn't sleep for the terror   of knowing there was a book of ghost stories downstairs

in the library   would burn all morning   all her own   like James' are relentlessly ambiguous
one believer   and another so honed   transparent as lightning   against a garden

that swerves   as a child   she lay dying   as a woman   full of leaves   in her own
it's love that steps into the hall   all in erasure   decked out in the latest   ivory, ecru, bone

# Miss Jéromette and the Clergyman

Wilkie Collins had a brother       accompanied       by a tall column of mist
who had loved only once       the gesture at the throat       as she, the mirror of

his love    will come back     for him     it was such a simple story       a woman
encountered in a garden          a garden, the summer of night       the foreign

edge on her speech pulled him in       and on we go     to her murder, then a woman
will know       how wrong she has been       and still walk to the station       ago

# Some Paintings of Ghosts

There are so few paintings of ghosts, which is really rather odd
since there at last they could be seen, could slightly live
in the visible, under glass

where all errance squares
and there's an end almost to the body you forgot

there's a body that runs on
out ahead of the one inevitably left behind

in the shock of recognition on the face of the dying

that, in a Rembrandt sketch, or I saw it once
in a painting by Ingres, though he had not
put it there.

# Some Ghosts in Paintings

*Atelier du peintre,* Gustave Courbet, 1855. At the far right edge, just coming through the door or perhaps from behind a mirror is a man who isn't there.

*Sea and Rain,* James McNeill Whistler, 1865. A human husk stepping carefully over something very fragile in the sky.

Frederic Bazille, *Rose Terrace (Terrace at Méric),* 1867. But where is the terrace? the trellis? the woman who sits at the very, very edge of the park bench, a mere sketch

a white dress

sat down

in a garden

Bazille died

in the Franco-Prussian War shot just before he turned 29 he saw her there and wanted to finish it but under the circumstances, had no idea what that would mean.

*Les Jardins des Tuileries,* Monet, 1876; first woman on the left, white dress, her head and chest bending too much into the world.

Edward Hopper, 1963, *Sunlight in an Empty Room.*

# Gravesend

My ended grove          my threaded shriek          drawn along
by swans straining at the same          Did you fall off the edge

and which          home carved from an egg          as if a little

trap door slowly spread through every room          ever this ready
the dead are hauling          a circus behind them in flames

# Gravesend

Gravesend is named after Mr. Silvaneous Grave
who in 1123 opened a store here
at the end of the road
leading from London to the sea.

No, London does not go to the sea.

So Gravesend is named after Mr. Albert Graves
who established a hotel at the first point
that boats turned in from the channel to go up the Thames.

No, he is dead.

And Gravesend is named for a preacher,
Euphonious Grave by name, who fell off a cliff
one night at just this spot. There are those who say
the waves carried him off, ablaze.

They are wrong.

Once we dreamt that a grave had an end,
that a life didn't just keep on growing and growing
until the grave stretched from here
to its clearance.

No, a grave is a grievance.

From the 17th through the 19th centuries
Gravesend was a principal harbor
from which emigrants left England
for Australia or North or South America

South Africa and India. It was a door
through which people fell into the sea.
I never returned.

Gravesend swings back and forth
like a window in the wind. It is named
for the fact that you never returned. It bears
the name of a man who disappeared in plain sight
in the town square on a sunny day.

# Gravesend

The name Gravesend comes from the words
"grafs-ham" meaning "the place at the end of the grove"

is a nave, is you walking out
into the sun
and the trees
surround
the things left behind  a grave

clears the air.

Gravesend is recorded in the *Domesday Book,* 1086, called Gravesham
which meant the home of a reeve or a lord, of a sleeve or a word, of a team

headed toward. The sill of a window or a door.

Gravesend is so named because at the height of the plague
they brought the bodies out here

and threw them into the sea. It wasn't as callous as it sounds, for by then
the grove was over and the sleeve, a town, and someone had learned

how to fashion a deadbolt from a series of thumbs
and so we dream to the sound, the slip, the click, the something that won't

ever quite shut. They blame the plague, the heart, the age. A grave
is a door laid flat in the earth, worked into a hinge, which articulates a gulf

without being a bridge.

# Interview Series 2

*Why is this town called Gravesend?*
*And what do you think of that name?*

Why is it called Gravesend? Now that you mention it, that's an interesting question. I've lived here all my life, and I've heard a lot of stories, but I don't know if any of them are true. What do I think of it as a name for a town? I've always rather liked it, actually; it makes me think of engravings and grayscales and all sorts of things to do with printing, but I doubt that has anything to do with the real history—but then history isn't real anyway, is it?

I'm starting my inquiries at the crown pub of the town, The Three Daws, crowded on a Friday at 8pm.

What do I think of it? I think it's pretty morbid actually. Hopeful? No, I don't really see how you could think of it as hopeful. Though it's better than Black Heath, I guess.

Kind of dismal isn't it? But our weather's great—hottest place in England at times. We broke the record two years ago.

What do I think of the name Gravesend? I quite like it actually. It has dignity.

Rather sad in a way isn't it?

I think it's morbid, but it's accurate.

The Three Daws is arguably the oldest pub on the Thames, and, as I've been reminded by at least five people in the village, it plays an important role in *Great Expectations*. I ask the barmaid what she thinks of the name Gravesend. Gravesend? It's a good name. It's in the *Domesday Book*. We used to have more pubs in this town than in any other town in England. Ghosts? You're writing a book on ghosts? This place is full of them. It's the oldest pub on the river. They say Pocahontas died here. No, I mean here, in this pub, that's what they say—and why not believe it? No, I've never seen a ghost, but I've heard one. I've been down here in the bar, and heard someone walking directly above me when I knew that no one could be up there. And bottles fly off the shelves sometimes, or chairs get up-ended. Everyone who works here has a different story; we all feel them.

It's in the *Domesday Book,* says Lester, the owner. There it's listed as Graff de Sham. A graff was a sheriff and sham meant home, so it's basically "the home of the sheriff." Several centuries of sloppy articulation could easily turn it into Gravesend. Ghosts? Give me a break.

At Waterloo Station in London, I was told I couldn't buy a round trip to Gravesend. Aren't coming back until Saturday, are you? No? Then the only ticket I can sell you is a one-way. Which train do you take? The one marked Gravesend—and don't worry, you can't miss it. It's the end of the line.

Can I ask you a question? (This time it's someone asking me.) Are you from Australia? No, from San Francisco. Can I ask *you* a question? What do you think of the name Gravesend? Horrible says one. Don't know, says the other, I've lived here all my life, and I've never really thought about it. You know why it's called that? Because so many people were buried here during the war. Which war? *The* war.

Enormous container ships float by in the background, headed for the docks at Tillbury across the river. During the plague, one person tells me, they'd bring all the bodies down to Tillbury, which was used as a huge morgue. That's why it's called that—get it? *Till Bury*—and then they'd ferry them across to Gravesend, and we'd bury them.

It's here, someone tells me, that all the apple orchards ended and the outskirts of London began.
*So?*
They were Gravensteins.

As if the grave could end, said a ship, this fog
is not among the listed                would have shifted in and out of light in a way most
unbecoming, it unbecame     and floated just inches over the water     was not found
in the morning.

Do you know why it's called Gravesend? Because for centuries, when ships arrived here from all over the world, everyone who had died on the journey—from cholera or dysentery or scurvy—were buried here because it was the first place they landed.

Because the plague stopped right before it got here, so no one was dying out here, so the graves ended.

It's because if you'd lined up, shoulder to shoulder, all the people who'd died of the plague in London, they would have reached to here.

If the grave would end, if all were a choir, if the mansion shattered, and a woman coming up the stairs disappeared. We see her all the time. She's usually calling out a name, but as soon as she sees us, she stops and looks afraid.

If you go up to the Railroad Tavern and look round the side, you'll see three graves lined up against the wall—those are the last three people to die of the plague. You know, we're mentioned in Dickens. The Three Daws Tavern is mentioned by name. Can't remember why; it's something to do with tunnels. There are tunnels under the whole town, and a lot of them start at the Three Daws. Smugglers used them, and people getting away from the press gangs. Press gangs? When a ship couldn't get enough sailors, they'd park offshore and send a couple men in to the taverns to get young guys drunk. Then they'd hit them over the head, drop them through a hole in the floor to a boat waiting below, and before you know it, you've got a career in the Navy.

You put an end to the grave, and then you end. Some slight slippage that streamed beneath. A rapt commerce in which none of the merchants is seen. And then there's that housing project just beyond the church. Was going great, but it's gotten bogged down because they hit a graveyard—it's an ancient one, and every time they come across more remains, they have to stop work and do the right thing.

You know Dickens' ghost haunts the graveyard up at Rochester Cathedral. He peers at all the gravestones—they say he's looking for his own. He wanted to be buried there, but they put him in Poet's Corner in Westminster Cathedral instead.

It's because so many people left from this port going to American or Canada or Australia and no one ever saw them again.

Dickens also haunts the Corn Exchange. He looks up at the clock, then takes out his watch and checks it against his own, and then turns and walks into the cathedral. He looks like a normal old man, so even though he's a ghost, can this be said to be a haunting?

You put an end to the grave
                                        and no one came. I stopped in a pub
whose walls are filled, top to bottom, with photos. One showed the whole town crowded into an alley around a feast, so numerous they spilled out the back, they overflowed. It's VE Day, the publican tells me, and the man who brought me the photo is right there in the picture somewhere.

Gravesend is strongly marked by its World War II past. The whole region was a principal target during the Battle of Britain, and over the airbase at Biggin Hill nearby, a phantom Spitfire still flies. It's never been seen, but it's often heard. Apparently it's a very distinctive sound, and sometimes, immediately after it has passed, low voices are heard, at times clinking glasses.

And there's a sailor who died in a harrowing storm just yards from the door of the inn where he would have found help for his foundering ship who has ever since continued his journey, struggling to the spot where he died, at which point he suddenly stands up straight and strides right into the place, now a pub, where he goes out like a light.

Ghosts are rarely calm, though there are some, standing in line to buy stamps, as if they traveled more lightly, over which you are still crying because of the body and its illegible beauty stitching a catch in the breath, and birds intervene. Some places are magnets, or maybe it's simply that habit is just as deep an emotion as terror or grief. Or that all habit is based, though often unconsciously, on joy; for example, Anne Boleyn continues to wander the grounds of Hever Castle, where she lived as a child, and was, as a child, very happy.

Fog starts collecting on the river, making the huge container vessels parked out there, waiting to go up to London, begin to dissolve, and a yacht or two—one named the Princess Pocahontas—begin to become a part of the landscape, which is turning blue and grey and cold. A dozen white swans float downstream in a line. They say you can't actually bury anybody here. What with a thirty foot tide and all this marsh, as soon as they stick them in the ground, they start to rise.

# Pocahontas (1595, Powhatan Confederacy—
1616, Gravesend, England)

So Pocahontas, lost in the graveyard, said to her husband,
so soften   the New World   is an edge   and returning

she turned around and saw him becoming
someone who used to live where she was dying.

Pocahontas once threw herself on the body of Captain John Smith to save him,
then married his colleague John Rolfe a few years later.

From the 17th to the 19th centuries, thousands and thousands of ships

is a windmill or threshold, a guildhall or swordhilt
is a windowsill struck by lightning, the huge sails

billowing out and the curtains

"I'm at that stage in life"
and then all that dancing on water.

Pocahontas died in Gravesend at the age of 22.
She was there to catch a boat back to Virginia
with her husband and child, who were going home.

So Pocahontas lost in the graveyard
a small charm that once depended
from a chain
around her ankle

        is one way to figure

the cost to her eyesight, to her continually flagrant
insistence upon dying as a demonstration
of the central role of irony in history
               .after all
                      that departure
the first Native American ever to visit Europe stayed forever. A fire
in 1727 destroyed the parish records, which included the location
of Pocahontas' grave, by nature, a door
                is a gap
                    but a ceiling
wouldn't be offered  in pieces  or things  that can't be divided, one cannot

for instance, offer another
a piece of grief or survival.

# The Ghost Dance

Emile Berliner, one of the first developers of the gramophone, recorded numerous Arapaho, Commanche, and Caddo ghost dances, as well as a Paiute gambling song, and published them in July, 1894.

*When from the door I saw him coming*

The Ghost Dance dates to 1888, when, based on a vision he had during a solar eclipse, the Paiute mystic Wovoka claimed the earth would soon end, and be therefore inherited, especially through dancing, in which one dies for a minute

*Then saw I      the many plainly*

Wovoka's vision of non-violent resistance was shared by Tolstoy: To you can no damage be, who turns again

*And saw that they, in numbers entering*

The ghost dances were recorded by the ethnologist James Mooney, who may in some cases also have played them.

*Entered calling their innumerable names*

Tolstoy published *The Kingdom of God is Within You* in 1894, in which the other cheek in which one sees

the Ghost Dance movement largely died out after Wounded Knee (December 29, 1890) in which some had believed

the Ghost Dance shirt is impervious to bullets

a rag flies around the sun at specific intervals

Thomas Edison filmed a Sioux ghost dance on September 24, 1894—or more precisely, he filmed a dance that featured true ghost dance costumes, but the documentation carefully states that it is not an authentic ghost dance bending as the light will not

It is 1894, and the gramophone is being sold in a shop in Baltimore. In fact, by fall, they will have sold over 1000 playing machines and 25,000 records, ashless are the voices                                                        we have become

that still    and faces fast       in which they turn and slowly halt
and latch you in the glance. The dance, brief and the ghost

lived within       whatever we were
was photographed with the lights out.

# The Name

The name Gravesend has nothing to do
with a grave or an end and there are

no pleasure craft out in the crowded harbor. The sails, sky-shaped in silicate
and built a loft that will not stop. There is nothing

for which you've been saving. They are boarding carrying
a single envelope and waving, or waving a handkerchief and ignoring

the historical significance of the waving of white things, pale in their faces, they are
wearing out in a wavering line along the deck and held in time only by the railing.

# Engraved

There was nothing in the grave. They cracked it open
and only the newspaper.

The grave came back. He stirred his tea with a finger
and glanced at the news.

There are no graves in Gravesend, which is of course
logical. And overflowed with it—

The relation of water to the dead

in which we washed our hands

in its liminal spaces—bridges, rivers,
shore upon shore and shoreline unfurling
the shadow around a person

was a shroud unwound and the tiny thing flying.

# Kent

In the grounds of Bayham Abbey     in a garden designed by Repton
a procession of monks just about dusk   or just after darkness has fallen
go walking.

Or there was no sadness, just a simple fold in time.

One must be for others a reason to live.

Often, it is said, the presence of a ghost is signaled by illogical cold.

Lord Halifax noted it when investigating "the Laughing Man of Wrotham," who strode
into his brother's room and murdered him   night after night

to the horror of the maid who, a century later, wedged a chair against the door and
watched him disappear.

There is no cure

for anything, and that cough you have, Madam, once

there was a fire every Friday the 13th, and once there was a death
that seemed to deserve it, but that was an illusion. Once there was a
death, but that was illusory, too. And all over Kent, someone is still
heading up the stairs, lighting the way with a match.

THREE

# WHAT DO YOU THINK A GHOST IS?

# Cicatrice


It's not the death that scars    but the grief    leapt    from the speeding train
and the young girl slain    by a shadow    (he'd hung himself)

or the one who took poison to stop thinking of it    he jumped overboard
from debt    we think an exit    from regret    there is no tightrope

on which she walked out    it was all her fault    that started walking
was not the killer but the killed    that made the incident    permanent

and the one who heard    the heart in all its heraldry    out flagging down the navy
or simply a baby    that couldn't be saved    is a sound held

by everyone on edge:    either, either    of no other    now unfettered touch

# Ghosts in the Sun

shine upon stone   a woman's fingers on the edge   of the overflowing fountain
watches                    the knot come undone            and the dog run headlong

after the birds, scattering them    beneath the tree    where deep in the shade
a man suddenly seems    not entirely there    and they gathered around him

to watch           reflections cross his face            as they often cross a pond


or the first ghost was the sun          and then it dies again          a white stain
on a slow eye       a boy lost      on a Ferris wheel      and then it dies in sheets

a spiral grave       with a hook-and-eye       deep in the shade of a burning tree

# Whole Ghost

From one horizon to the other      who counted their faces      all in attendance
a whole country      stained like a portrait      into a sheet    held up to the light

Ghosts appear in place of whatever a given people will not face      There are days
the entire sky is a ghost      though again      it's not necessarily what you'd think

bright sun      full of birds      you're in a park      and everything in sight is alive

# Traveling Ghost

To bury the heart in one land and the hands in another  says the legend  the heart is always
buried alone no matter what        you buried              the heart              is a grave

in the legend    is an hour invented     and here the long       road lined with poplars

I have a friend    who draws nothing but clouds.   As they speed across France, nothing
is lost from view. The train was invented   to shred a sun, to carefully cut the blind spots out

and everything that once was light came along.                    The sun is always alone

while the heart has all of France

like a stone              under the tongue          and like a stone under the tongue
it stays aloft    despite          which buries itself like    a face in its hands.   What you see

from a train      is what has escaped      a simple operation      a by-pass for instance

in which they take out the heart and lay it on a table.      I have a friend who had the job
of holding the hearts at certain points in the procedure. They'd literally  She said actually

exactly                    the weight you'd think they'd be                  intuitively
trace its meridian with a fingernail and compass   replace the map with a razor and an anchor

It often saved their lives and you look up to find that you've buried your friends in your hands

66

# Crowds

The man simply walked through her she said        she saw him coming and felt
at an intersection        standing on a corner        a man slipped

a century, and the woman        sensed his fingers    "inside my chest"    a caress
of which I think he was completely unaware   he never even saw me   until he passed

and then was scared.    And silently        trailing through me     will you ever be
a sound in an empty house        an inexplicable mark that, washed off, grows dark

# And Are Ghosts

also inextricably linked to snow     three days it took her    to get across Nebraska
and the whole time       there he was    her grandfather        in the passenger seat

refusing to be frightening    and tried to hold him     as he came closer    and more
the snow, the farther        the body came to be          his heartbeat of her sobbing

at the side of the road     at his funeral    as the censer swung over      she alone saw
the small wind as it started  snowing her grandmother said  walking out of the church

I would have thought    he had already gone    at every snowfall in her uncanny silence
she thinks with the help    of his haunting she may someday      without the falling

# Interview Series 3

*What do you think ghosts are?*
*Do you think you'll ever be one?*

I don't know... I think they're communication, simply that; a ghost is simply a connection.

And then she goes on to mention some rather odd occurrences—hundreds of red beetles all over the kitchen the day her mother died, and for a year after her son-in-law's death, she kept seeing his car go by.
Do I think I'll ever be one? I'd like to be; it seems, if nothing else, like a way to get on with it.

I think they're entities stuck in time. We the "living" pass right on through it, along it, along with it, and then in dying, if all goes well, we pass out of it, but ghosts get stuck, locked, are left half-in and half-out. It hurts. Become one? I hope not.

What is a ghost? It's something that hides behind doors (said without irony)—ghosts *lurk;* that is their defining quality. Will I ever become one? Quite possibly.

A ghost is that which exceeds the four elements, what will not fit within. Which suggests them as excess, which has by definition nowhere to go, that might show up anywhere, a little startled, a shade persistent, an average shadow that doesn't move with the sun. Will I ever become one? Certainly not.

A ghost is that which refuses to go on—they're comfortable with death.

Or a ghost is burned into the sky as an image is burned onto the retina of an eye. It was an accident, or at least incidental; it was nothing special, but stayed too long and so remains emblazoned on a certain patch of air, annealed there, watching, for instance, for a ship to sail into view.

They are laws of physics caught at that fractional moment of suspension that all laws pass through as they're changing. Yes, I think the laws of physics change all the time, but because we're completely bound by them, we can't remember their ever having been different; however, we can perceive the glitches that persist if the revision isn't fast enough, and sometimes, no doubt, we are the glitch, and have no idea of it.

What is a ghost? It's tangled electricity. It's a radiogram of the air, an ex-ray of the sky.

What is a ghost? Well, that's tantamount to asking what you think the present is. We have a much clearer take on both the past and the future than we do on the present—it remains a gap between two clarities, a void, and as such, it cannot possibly make sense, at which point, we must admit that we are lacking crucial information on our own state, and therefore can't even begin to comment on the state of other entities that are not attached to the present, even though they may be visible from it. Will I ever be one? I might very well be one now, if viewed from another state.

I get up and turn on the light.

A ghost is one life layered upon another that has not yet been named.
A ghost is a crossroads, now mobile, as in the Middle Ages, avoided at night, the air thickening there, but the intersection itself, invisible up close, and suddenly warm and at home.

A ghost is a broken window, though the window does not end the room; it only breaks the seal.

What is a ghost? It's the spirit returning to exact revenge. Will I return? I don't know—I suppose it will depend on how much pain I'm in.

A ghost bit a child of the tip of her thumb          And the child replaced the sun.
It seems that great emotion disrupts the structure that makes time and space appear separate.

Or a ghost is a knot in the otherwise smooth flow of time, an electrical storm in a jewelry box, grief perfectly aligned. And sometimes a ghost is a shared thing; sometimes the entire population of a city or country will just happen to look in the mirror at the same time, and from then on there was a city in the sky, as all cities are if we consider that the sky reaches to the ground, and this city, too, thought it was alive, and the candles walked off by themselves.

# Old Wives' Tales

*Whatever you do is forever done*

and will mark the house
and the bird in the fire

and will come back on them
who stain or find themselves

who simply walk in
don't look in the mirror

you think you sell your soul
it's the little block of space

and the house the town
that little tower

who enter centuries later
that can't wash off

don't open the jar
the house that rides a flame to shore

but it's not yours; it's air
in which you stand that dies

# Freud Claims

it's the unburied inside
Grief is a machine

who come back unloving
that must be assembled correctly

You are standing in the light
and I am late.

while the light shines through you
You are there in the doorway

and the door is closed
You are walking down a hill

and I am going home
and I watch you from a window

I am running down the stairs

like a little gear in a tear

# Some Chinese Ghosts

after Lafcadio Hearn

*for Keith Waldrop*

if the rose is made of phosphor
if for a single shoe

the ghosts of China
the morally errant, the cruel

all along the northern road
which left alive

and the hundred smaller bells
the wind becomes a hound

are rarely evil, are not the restless
so the fire sprang back to life

among the hundred flying oaks
one or two who changed

# Across

If there was light on a building   if the building was white   if the light in a wash
passed a hand across a face         washed the light right off             I sat across

from a building across which            the sun in setting        a summer so slowly
made itself a path.        If light were, as some say                  the ghost of God

what house would                 stand in the middle of the street listing names
and would they all add up    and could we then all stop      I watch light cross

a building               and make of it a face          I watch the façade
of a building                       build itself to sight                        slight

wound to the eye       the sort that leaves the light inside                sealed

# Ghosts

are houses.      (The places we exceed ourselves can live.)     And every house

is a guest.    I live in an old one.    I watch it move.    "I am moved," I say

at inappropriate times. And then must say "I'm sorry"    though not to whom

## Who Did

not see                because to see          is to enter as
a child on a staircase               an inherited streetlight

but the child's hand is on the light switch    in fascination
will flick it                 will it              to be alive

a thing must turn around and smile            or
we will not will it                 to be a child

one must stand        on the bottom stair      or on
the top          and be struck        by the emptiness

of a house                   in which they're all asleep

# After This Death There Will Be No Other

Some say a child          becomes the house          some houses hold
the child in hand          in the heart of a bird          is its hollow home

that green flight that lets the house lose form          where was the room
why a door to the air          why air in the eye          and why

only sky there          the child held the house          in the palm of her hand
and the sky poured over it          painting her out

# Haint Blue

On the frame around the porch where its edges        or ashes        or an eyelash
of feathering porchlight     quietly annihilates darkness    all throughout Georgia

the frames are painted this particular shade     because it keeps the ghosts away   or
keeps them closer, curled up  in the home     I can't remember    which one was first

to point out    the robin's egg laid     on the third storey windowsill    on the inside
a bird  born within the house  of such a deep blue that we've never been able to find it

# One No

When this it goes.      She said winnow winnow      Why come thou      Watch now
My latch was its watchspring      My love was an eland      And I that hypnotic

am knocking on tables   unmarrowed in craving   the chant won't ungiving   a knuckle
a breastbone   a light switch, an ibis   They say that wherever   bird enter—when there

as it happens, a bird comes into the house uninvited      (most often through a window)
someone will die soon.   My lover, that eon   My watcher, that whiteness   That bone there

an icon   I stumble to seem like      I stutter and bleach eye      and sinew on farther
which unlike further   means a distance you can measure      and my boat such a small one

# How Might a Ghost Age

The error in the mirror is living a glove   And at that  the vision seemed to give way
to something less   as if seen through glass upon rain   let's stay   he said stay  and

I will answer your questions he said there is     an answer and I am every     nearly
and your patience may       from a crack in the hour       or untraceable crevasse

so fundamentally different from     the damage to which we've grown accustomed:
age, pox, rust, fright, the light           that broke it                 came from inside

# Who Walked

across water        who gathered        there over        a gathering mist
is a migration.        They went down just off the coast        and sometimes almost

an army balanced out there on the waves        but in rags        and flagrant in wind
Legend claims that on calm nights    you can hear their footsteps from the cliff    a soft

howl, the children are wading out past the horizon    he was sailing alone   returning late
when he saw an army of children    dressed in rage   walking over the sea on their hands

# The Ghost Orchid

actually exists    the proper name    of an excised space
a suddenly arboreal egret    in pieces    the entire

choir    in an instant of amnesia    sang a tune
my four-year-old sings    that he calls his angel song

it's composed    of the single word "window"    over
and over    the dead    unlike us    do not live alone

# Acknowledgements

I would like to thank the editors, publishers, and curators of the following journals and websites for their generosity in publishing some of these poems, in some cases, in earlier versions.

*Almost Island*
*Caffeine Destiny*
*Chimera*
*Coconut*
*The Colorado Review*
*Common Place*
*Conjunctions*
*The Denver Quarterly*
*Drunken Boat*
*Eleven Eleven*
*Harper Palate*
*Lana Turner*
*Mimesis*
*Mipoesias*
*Neue Rundschau*
*The New Review of Literature*
*/nor*
*Sidebrow*
*Slightly West*
*Upstairs at Duroc*
*Vacarme*
*Van Gogh's Ear*
*Zen Monster*

And many, many thanks to Aaron Belz for publishing a number of these as the chapbook *Ghosts are Hope* through his press Observable Books.

# Notes

The interviewees for the first and third interviews were Omar Berrada, Marie Borel, Vincent Broqua, Rémi Bouthonnier, Norma Cole, Martin Corless-Smith, Jennifer K. Dick, Suzanne Doppelt, Alan Ereira, Sarah Ereira, Safaa Fathy, Jean Frémon, Jeremy Hayward, Mary-Virginia Langston, Jessica Munns, Mel Nichols, Sarah Riggs, Joe Ross, Ryoko Sekiguchi, Donna Stonecipher, and Leslie Taylor, though not in that order, and not in the exact words used here. The interviewees for the second interview were various people living in the town of Gravesend, Kent, England in the summer of 2008; I did not take their names, and I have not used their exact words.

The title "After This Death There Will Be No Other" is taken from the last line of Dylan Thomas' poem "On the Death of a Child by Fire." The stories evoked, with liberties taken, in section two include *The True Relation of the Apparition of One Mrs. Veal* by Daniel Defoe, *A Chapter in the History of a Tyrone Family* by Sheridan Le Fanu, *The Friend of the Family* by Henry James, and *Miss Jéromette and the Clergyman* by Wilkie Collins.

I owe the title "Ajar" to that brilliant poet Kokoy Guevara.

I apologize for the grammatical error in the last line of the poem "Ghost Stories"; the clause should read "I hanged myself," not "I hung myself," but I couldn't stand to give up the rhyme.

NEW CALIFORNIA POETRY

| | |
|---|---|
| *edited by* | Robert Hass<br>Calvin Bedient<br>Brenda Hillman<br>Forrest Gander |

*For,* by Carol Snow

*Enola Gay,* by Mark Levine

*Selected Poems,* by Fanny Howe

*Sleeping with the Dictionary,* by Harryette Mullen

*Commons,* by Myung Mi Kim

*The Guns and Flags Project,* by Geoffrey G. O'Brien

*Gone,* by Fanny Howe

*Why/Why Not,* by Martha Ronk

*A Carnage in the Lovetrees,* by Richard Greenfield

*The Seventy Prepositions,* by Carol Snow

*Not Even Then,* by Brian Blanchfield

*Facts for Visitors,* by Srikanth Reddy

*Weather Eye Open,* by Sarah Gridley

*Subject,* by Laura Mullen

*This Connection of Everyone with Lungs,* by Juliana Spahr

*The Totality for Kids,* by Joshua Clover

*The Wilds,* by Mark Levine

*I Love Artists,* by Mei-mei Berssenbrugge

*Harm.,* by Steve Willard

*Green and Gray,* by Geoffrey G. O'Brien

*The Age of Huts (compleat),* by Ron Silliman

*Selected Poems, 1974–2006: it's go in horizontal,* by Leslie Scalapino

*rimertown/an atlas,* by Laura Walker

*Ours,* by Cole Swensen

*Virgil and the Mountain Cat: Poems,* by David Lau